AF269759

OXFORD BOOKWORMS LIBRARY
*Factfiles*

# Usain Bolt

ALEX RAYNHAM

Stage 1 (400 headwords)

Series Editor: Rachel Bladon
Founder Factfiles Editor: Christine Lindop

Great Clarendon Street, Oxford, OX2 6DP, United Kingdom

Oxford University Press is a department of the University of Oxford.
It furthers the University's objective of excellence in research, scholarship,
and education by publishing worldwide. Oxford is a registered trade
mark of Oxford University Press in the UK and in certain other countries

© Oxford University Press 2019

The moral rights of the author have been asserted

First published 2019

10 9 8 7 6 5 4 3



**No unauthorized photocopying**

All rights reserved. No part of this publication may be reproduced,
stored in a retrieval system, or transmitted, in any form or by any means,
without the prior permission in writing of Oxford University Press, or as
expressly permitted by law, by licence or under terms agreed with the
appropriate reprographics rights organization. Enquiries concerning
reproduction outside the scope of the above should be sent to the ELT
Rights Department, Oxford University Press, at the address above

You must not circulate this work in any other form and you must
impose this same condition on any acquirer

Links to third party websites are provided by Oxford in good faith and
for information only. Oxford disclaims any responsibility for the materials
contained in any third party website referenced in this work



ISBN: 978 0 19 463426 7

A complete recording of this Bookworms edition of *Usain Bolt* is available.

Printed in China

Word count (main text): 5,494

For more information on the Oxford Bookworms Library,
visit www.oup.com/elt/gradedreaders



ACKNOWLEDGEMENTS

*Cover image by*: Getty Images/Salih Zeki Fazlioglu/Anadolu Agency.

*The publisher would like to thank the following for the permission to reproduce photographs:*
Alamy Stock Photo pp.7 (sports day/Eye Ubiquitous), 9 (Downtown Falmouth, Jamaica/John
A Allen, Jr.), 10 (Falmouth, Jamaica/robertharding), 16 (Kingston/robertharding), 32 (Jamaican
Men's 4 x 100m Relay team/ZUMA Press, Inc.), 37 (Usain Bolt/East News sp. z o.o.), 38 (Usain and
parents Wellesley and Jennifer Bolt/Andrew Rowland); Getty Images pp.iv (100m final 2016/
Alexander Hassenstein), 2 (Bolt victorious/Robert Beck/Sports Illustrated), 4 (Wellesley Bolt/
Simon Bruty/Sports Illustrated), 6 (Waldensia primary school running track/Mark Guthrie/
Contour), 6 (Waldensia primary school/Mark Guthrie/Contour), 9 (William Knibb Memorial High
School/Ian Walton), 11 (Michael Johnson/Mark Sandten), 12 (crowd/Bernard Weil/Toronto Star),
14 (Bolt 2002/Andy Lyons), 15 (rising star/Michael Steele), 18 (Bolt & Glen Mills/Michael Steele),
19 (Bolt training/Michael Steele), 21 (Mens 100m 2008/Victah Sailer), 22 (Beijing Olympics/
Joe Rimkus Jr./Miami Herald/MCT), 23 (Bolt 2008/Philippe Perusseau/Icon Sport), 24 (Bolt with
time/Adrian Dennis/AFP), 24 (Bolt & mother/Robert Beck/Sports Illustrated), 25 (Bolt celebrates
win/Mike Hewitt), 27 (Bolt with photographers/Olivier Morin/AFP), 27 (Bolt after winning gold/
Julian Finney), 28 (Bolt on stage/Simon Bruty/Sports Illustrated), 30 (Yohan Blake/Michael Steele),
30 (false start/Olivier Morin/AFP), 31 (Jamaica Olympic team 2012/Lars Baron), 34 (Bolt speaking/
Adrian Dennis/AFP), 35 (Bolt celebrating/Donald Miralle/Sports Illustrated), 35 (relay medal
ceremony/Patrick Smith), 36 (Bolt with gold medal/Laurence Griffiths), 39 (Bolt with kids/Toru
Yamanaka/AFP), 40 (Sherwood Content sign/Jewel Samad/AFP), 41 (Bolt playing football/Lynne
Cameron), 46 (Wellesley and Jennifer Bolt/Fred Duval/FilmMagic), 46 (Nugent Walker/Dave
J Hogan), 46 (Glen Mills/Ian Walton), 46 (Yohan Blake/Cameron Spencer), 58 (Cathy Freeman/
Jeff Haynes/AFP); Reuters News Agency, Thomson Reuters p.33 (Bolt & Bailey/Sergio Moraes);
Shutterstock pp.3 (map of Jamaica/Ingo Menhard), 44 (Caribbean map/Peter Hermes Furian).



REFERENCES

1 *Faster than Lightning: My Story*, Usain Bolt with Matt Allen, HarperSport, 2013, p.146
2 *Faster than Lightning: My Story* (Bolt with Allen, 2013), p.153
3 *Athletics – Men's 200m Final – Beijing 2008 Summer Olympic Games*, 20th August 2008, retrieved
September 2018 from https://www.youtube.com/watch?v=QUpC71WbAhA

# CONTENTS

# 1 Lightning Bolt

It is 14ᵗʰ August 2016, before the final of the Olympic men's 100 metres, in Rio de Janeiro. Eight runners come out onto the track: they are the fastest men in the world. There are 60,000 people in the stadium, and many of them want one man to win: Usain Bolt, from Jamaica.

Usain Bolt walks up and down the track, and people begin calling his name. Many runners do not smile much or talk before a race – but Usain looks happy, and laughs, and does a dance for the cameras.

Soon, the runners are ready. Everyone is waiting for the start of the race now, and the stadium is quiet.

When the race begins, Usain Bolt is behind at first, but he goes past three runners in the first four seconds! He is now moving at more than forty kilometres an hour, and after seven seconds, the race is between him and American Justin Gatlin.

Usain Bolt goes in front, and he wins by 0.08 seconds. In the stadium, thousands of people get up onto their feet. Usain opens his arms to them and runs along the track with a big smile on his face. Then he takes off his running shoes and does his famous 'lightning bolt' pose. Everyone shouts and cheers: Usain Bolt is perhaps the most famous runner of all time, and one of the greatest people in any sport. And because he loves talking and laughing with people, they love him, too.

The 'lightning bolt' pose,
Rio de Janeiro, 2016

# 2 A village boy

Usain Bolt was born on 21st August 1986, in Sherwood Content – a quiet village in Jamaica. After Usain learned to walk, he did not stop moving. He went around and around the family house, and he never sat down. Usain's mother and father could not understand it. *Is something wrong with him?* they thought.

Sherwood Content was a nice village for a young boy. The houses had gardens with beautiful, tall trees around them. The weather in Jamaica is usually hot and sunny, so the people of Sherwood Content often sat in front of their houses and talked. Children played in the gardens and along the quiet roads.

Usain's father Wellesley worked for a Jamaican coffee business. He went all around Jamaica for his work, and often came home late, after Usain was in bed. For her work, Usain's mother Jennifer made dresses for people, at home. When Usain was little, he often watched her, and soon he helped her with the dresses, too.

Usain's father was very strict: he got angry when Usain did not work hard, or do the right thing. When Usain was young, Wellesley liked him to stay at home with his mother. But Usain often wanted to go out, and his mother did not stop him. Usain took the family dog Brownie and ran here and there between the tall trees of Sherwood Content, with no shoes on his feet. Sometimes he went to his Aunt Lilly's house, because she always gave him something nice to eat. Then he ran home before his father arrived back.

People in Usain's village got their water from the river – and Usain carried all the water for his family. Every week, he needed to carry a bucket to the river and back forty-eight times. But Usain did not want to walk to the river again and again. So he began to carry two buckets every time. It was very hard work, but young Usain was very tall, and his arms, legs, and back were soon very strong.

At school, Usain was a happy, friendly boy, and he liked to have fun. He had a lot of friends, but his best friend was Nugent Walker Junior, or 'NJ'. NJ, Usain, and Usain's brother Sadiki loved playing football and cricket. Usain was very good at cricket, and he wanted to be a cricketer when he was older. He began playing cricket for his school when he was only eight years old – most of the players were eleven!

Usain could run very fast, and when he was eight, a teacher called Mr Nugent saw this. He wanted Usain to run in a race at sports day. Sports day is one of the most important days in the Jamaican school year, because many Jamaicans love sport. Everyone races on sports

Usain's school in Sherwood Content, with the running track

day – or watches the races and cheers for their friends. *Win the 100 metres at sports day*, Mr Nugent told Usain, *and you can have a nice box of Jamaican food.* Usain liked his food, and when he heard this, he wanted to win. But Ricardo Geddes was in the race, too – and he was the fastest boy in the school.

When it was sports day, lots of people came and watched the 100 metres race. Usain did not want to lose in front of all his friends – and he wanted that box of food, too.

When he began running, Usain was suddenly very excited. It felt *good*. At first, Ricardo was not far behind him. But soon, Usain's long legs carried him away, and he could not hear Ricardo. He ran faster and faster, and finished first. He was the winner – and he now knew something important. He liked being Number One. He liked it a lot. Later, Mr Nugent gave Usain his box of food – and he liked that, too!

Sports day: one of the most important days in the Jamaican school year

# 3    An athlete

After Usain beat Ricardo Geddes, he began running for his school team in races for children from the towns and villages near Sherwood Content. Then he ran in the 100 metres and 150 metres at his first national championships – races for children from all over Jamaica. In the championships, Usain needed to do well in the heats – the races before the final. Only the best athletes from the heats can go into the finals.

Usain went through his heats OK. He did not win in the finals, but he ran well. Sports teachers from some of the high schools (bigger schools for children from when they are twelve or thirteen years old) watched his races and were interested in him. He was a very good runner, they saw.

Because of this, in 1998, when he was twelve years old, Usain started at William Knibb High School. It was a good school, and great at sport – and it was in Falmouth, a town by the sea not far from Sherwood Content.

Usain wanted to play cricket at William Knibb, but the school's coaches – their sports teachers – wanted him to train for the 200 and 400 metres. They did not want him to do the 100 metres, because he was very tall, and tall people often get a slower start in races. So he could not easily win a quick race, his coaches thought.

William Knibb High School

Falmouth, Jamaica

Usain began to run some very fast times, and sometimes the coaches at William Knibb could not believe them. When a new coach started at the school one day, Usain had to run races for him again and again. *My watch is wrong*, the coach thought, every time!

But Usain did not like training. When he trained for the 400 metres, he needed to run very far, very fast, many times. He often felt ill after. He did many exercises with his coaches, too – and he did one exercise called sit-ups 700 times a day! Because Usain did not like all the running and exercises, he began going into Falmouth town after school, at training time, and playing video games there with his friends. He wanted to have fun after a long school day, not run and do exercises.

One day, when Usain did not come to training, his coach, Pablo McNeil, went into Falmouth and found him. McNeil was an old Jamaican Olympic athlete, so he knew all about training hard. He wanted Usain to work more, to get stronger, and to be the best. Usain could win lots of races easily. But because he did not train hard, he did not get better.

**Falmouth town**

When Usain was thirteen, something changed for him. A boy called Keith Spence, from a different school, began beating Usain in every race – because he trained very hard. Usain did not like that, and after he lost to Spence again in 2000, he thought, *It's not going to happen next time*. So Usain began training harder.

One more important thing happened to Usain that year, too. At that time, people in Sherwood Content could not easily watch sport on television. But that summer, Usain saw a video of Michael Johnson at the Atlanta Olympics in 1996. He watched when Johnson won the 200 metres and the 400 metres, and got his gold medals. Usain saw the thousands and thousands of people in the Olympic stadium, and he thought, *This is exciting*. Now *he* wanted to win Olympic medals, too – and be the next Michael Johnson.

Usain began to work harder, and soon he was stronger and faster. When Usain raced Keith Spence again in 2001, he went past Spence in the first one hundred metres of their 200 metres race, then left him far behind!

Michael Johnson,
Atlanta, 1996

# 4    Champion!

In 2001, Usain's school coaches took him to Kingston, Jamaica for 'Champs', the biggest school athletics championships in the Caribbean. Champs is very important: 30,000 people watch the races every day in the National Stadium, and many watch the five-day championships on TV, too. Schools sing, dance, and cheer for their athletes, and everyone gets very excited!

Usain was only fourteen, and it was his first time at Champs, but he won the 400 metres. It was a great race, and he beat the national under-16s champion! He came second for William Knibb High School in the 200 metres, too. These were wonderful championships for Usain, and suddenly lots of people were interested in him.

Crowds at Champs

After Champs, the Jamaican national team wanted to take Usain to international races – races for people from all around the world. So in April 2001, he left Jamaica for the first time, and went to the Carifta Games in Barbados. He was excited at first, but he did not like being away from his mother and father, and his home.

The next year, Usain ran in the 200 and 400 metres at the Carifta Games in Nassau, the Bahamas. He raced the best young athletes in the Caribbean, and he won his races – and broke the Carifta Games records. These were great wins, and the crowd in Nassau loved him. They stood and cheered 'Lightning Bolt! Lightning Bolt!' Usain felt wonderful – and he liked the name 'Lightning Bolt' a lot!

Usain began training for some important races in the summer. The World Junior Championships were for young people from all around the world, but in 2002, they were in Kingston, Jamaica, and Usain's coach Pablo McNeil wanted him to go.

In the championships, Usain went through his heats easily. He felt good before the 200 metres final. But then he walked out into the stadium, and people called 'Bolt! Bolt! Lightning Bolt!' Usain was the only Jamaican in the final – and suddenly, he felt very afraid. These people were his fans – they liked him and wanted him to win. He did not want to lose in front of them. And because this was an under-20s race, and Usain was only fifteen, some of the runners were three or four years older than him. He began putting his running shoes on the wrong feet because he could not think!

Everyone started before Usain. But then something happened. He began running faster and faster – and he began going past people, too! In the last fifty metres, he was in front of everyone. He won the race by about two metres: he was the new World Junior Champion!

**World Junior Championships, Kingston, 2002**

Usain could not believe it at first. He looked around the stadium, and thousands of people cheered and called his name. Someone gave him a Jamaican flag, and he stood on the track with the flag around him. He was a champion, and it felt wonderful!

Usain was famous in Jamaica after that day, and the race taught him something big, too. Before the race, Usain felt very afraid – but he won it. He was strong, and he knew that now.

After the World Junior Championships, a car drove Usain from the airport home to Sherwood Content, and people stood along the road and waved and cheered. He was a national hero!

People around the world were interested in Usain now, too. Later that year, he won an award for the best new young athlete from the IAAF, a very big athletics organization. He went to Monaco, near France, for the award. Nobody went with him, and when he went back to Jamaica, his plane was late, so he needed to stay in a hotel in London for a night. He was only sixteen years old, and he was very afraid. He did not sleep all night – he sat on the bed with his bag because he wanted to go home, and he did not want the plane to go without him!

**Usain with his IAAF Award**

# 5 Injury

Usain's father was often angry with him because he did not work very hard at school. But with a little help, he did better in his last year at school and got into university. Because Usain won many medals that year, some American universities wanted him to train and run for them in the USA. But Usain did not want to leave Jamaica, and in 2003, he went to be a sports student at a university in Kingston. Kingston was about 150 kilometres away from Sherwood Content, so he lived there with a family friend.

Usain's new coach in Kingston was great, but Usain was not happy – the training was not right for him, he thought. It was very hard, and his body did not feel good. Usain talked to many people about it – but nobody listened to him.

In April 2004, Usain broke the world junior 200 metres record at the Carifta Games. But two weeks later, he got a bad leg injury, and his coach took him to Dr Müller-Wohlfahrt, a famous sports doctor in Germany.

Usain got his injury because he had scoliosis, Müller-Wohlfahrt said. When you have scoliosis, you have a bend in your back – and because of this, Usain's left leg was longer than his right leg. The scoliosis was very bad, Müller-Wohlfahrt said.

The doctor helped Usain with his back, and Usain slowly began to train again. But he had lots of injuries and could not race for months. In August, Usain went with the Jamaican team to the 2004 Athens Olympics, but he was not ready for the races. When he came fifth in his 200 metres heat and did not get into the final, people wrote bad things about him in the Jamaican newspapers. *Why didn't he do better?* they asked.

After Athens, Usain moved to a different athletics club in Kingston because he wanted to work with the famous coach Glen Mills. Mills worked his young athletes hard, but he listened to them and talked to them about their training. Different people needed to train differently, and Mills understood that.

Usain needed three years of training, Mills thought. He could run in some international races, Mills said.

But because he had scoliosis, he must work slowly, race carefully, and be 100% ready for 2008 – the next Olympic year.

Mills changed Usain's training a lot. Mills wanted Usain to be very strong, so six days a week, Usain first did lots of exercises, and then he trained on the track for hours. Later, at home, Usain did more exercises for his back and legs – and Mills came to his house every evening and watched! Mills and Usain watched Usain's race videos again and again, too, and talked about them. *How did Usain run? What did he need to change?*

Sometimes, Usain did not work hard in training – or he went out in Kingston and stayed out late, and did not come to the track. Mills did not get angry with him. He came to Usain's house, and talked to him. Mills was interested in Usain the person – not only Usain the athlete. The work was never easy, when Usain trained with Mills. But they were soon good friends. They trained hard, but they could relax and laugh, too.

An athlete must 'want something', Mills said, or they cannot train hard day after day and year after year. *What do you want?* he asked. Usain thought about this a lot. He wanted to be the best, and he wanted to make money and help his mother and father. Only the world's best athletes made a lot of money. Sometimes, Usain saw Jamaican runner Asafa Powell in Kingston. Powell was a great runner, and he had the 100 metres world record. He got lots of money when he won races, and he drove an expensive car. Usain wanted those things, too. So he needed to work hard.

Usain training

# 6      A new race

All through 2005 and 2006, Usain worked very hard with Coach Mills – and slowly, he got stronger. At that time, his training was for the 200 metres only. But Mills wanted him to train for the 400 metres, too.

Usain was not happy about that. He wanted to do the 100 metres, not the 400 metres. Usain was not right for the 100 metres, Mills thought, because he was very tall – but Usain asked again and again. *Break the Jamaican national record for the 200 metres,* Mills said in the end, *and you can run the 100 metres.*

And so, at the Jamaican Championships in 2007, Usain broke the 200 metres record! He finished that race in 19.75 seconds. Now he was the fastest 200 metres runner in Jamaica – and he did not need to do the 400 metres!

So that July, Usain ran the 100 metres for the first time at some championships in Rethymno, Greece. Coach Mills was very strict with him again. *You must run faster than 10.30 seconds,* he said, *or you need to begin training for the 400 metres.* Usain did not want that!

The race started, and Usain ran and ran – and when he came to the finish, he was in front. Then he looked up at the clock. 10.03 seconds – a wonderful time! Mills was excited, and Usain was very happy – no 400 metres for him now!

After nearly three years with Coach Mills, Usain was injury-free, and he felt good. At the first championships of 2008, Usain ran well. Then, in May, he raced Tyson Gay, the 100 metres World Champion, in the 100 metres in New York.

Usain got a great start, and after thirty metres, he looked across at Gay. Usain was in front! Usain ran hard to the finish. He wanted to win the race, and he did not think about his time at first – but when he finished and looked at the clock, he could not believe it! 9.72 seconds – it was a new world record! Mills ran to Usain and put his arms around him. It was only Usain's fifth 100 metres race, but now he was the fastest man in the world!

Usain and Tyson Gay, New York, 2008

# 7 The Beijing Olympics

In July 2008, when Usain went to China for the Beijing Olympic Games, he made a video on his phone. 'I'm going to Beijing,' he said in the video. 'I'm going to run fast, I'm going to win three gold medals, I'm going to come home a hero.'[1]

When Usain arrived at the Games, most track athletes knew him. But he was not world-famous: he could walk around the Olympic village, train quietly, relax, and play video games with his friends on the team, and people did not stop him for photos.

Beijing Olympics, 2008

This was not his first visit to Asia, and he liked it there because he had a lot of fans. But for Usain, Chinese food was too different from Jamaican food. So he began eating chicken nuggets from the fast-food shop in the Olympic village. He ate five boxes of chicken nuggets every day!

Usain went through his 100 and 200 metres heats easily. Then the big day came: the men's 100 metres final. Usain needed to beat the best 100 metres athletes in the world, and 91,000 people were in the Olympic stadium that day. Two more Jamaican athletes were in the final, too – Michael Frater and Asafa Powell. 'This is going to be a good race,' Usain told Powell before the start. 'Jamaica one and two. Let's go.'[2]

Richard Thompson from Trinidad got the best start, but after fifty metres, Usain went past everyone. Then, when he was in front, he relaxed and opened his arms. *Look at me!* that said. He was slower when he finished the race because of this, but it was a great time. 9.69 seconds – faster than his world record in New York!

Usain wins the 100 metres, Beijing

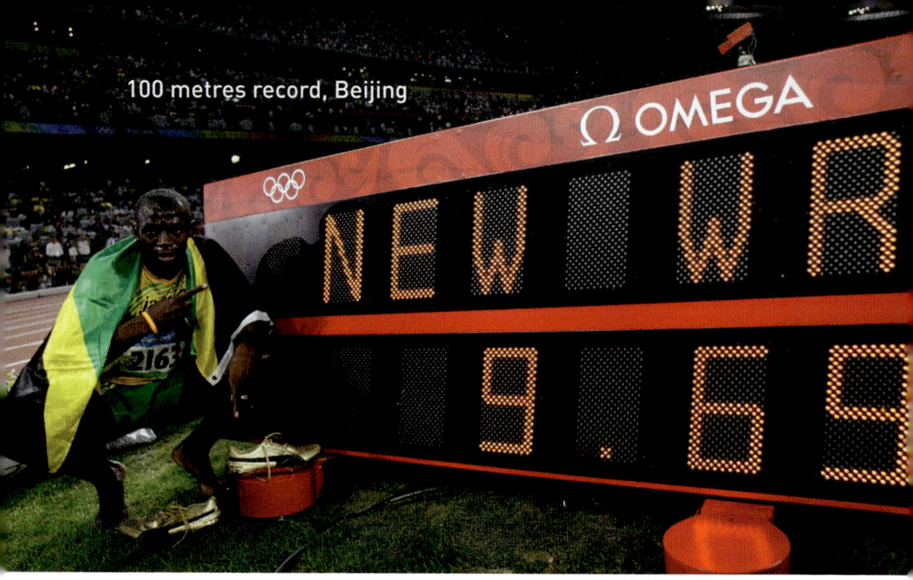

100 metres record, Beijing

Usain ran across the track, and the crowd cheered and waved. Suddenly, there were photographers all around him, so he opened his arms, and did his lightning bolt pose for the first time. Everyone loved it!

Then Usain went and found his mother and the Jamaican team in the crowd. Everyone was happy and excited for him. Back home in Kingston, Jamaica, people danced in the streets, and in Sherwood Content, Usain's Aunt Lilly ran excitedly around and around her house!

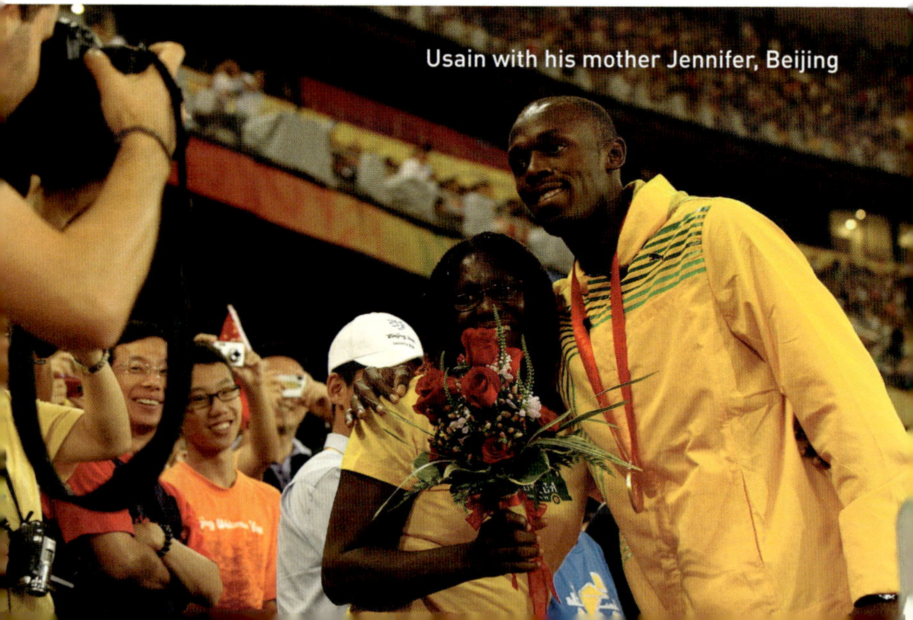
Usain with his mother Jennifer, Beijing

When Usain went back to the Olympic village that night, there was a crowd in front of the Jamaican building. 'Do the lightning bolt!' someone called. They all wanted photos with him. He could not walk quietly around the Olympic village after that, because everyone wanted to meet him.

Usain was more relaxed about the 200 metres final, four days later. The 100 metres was new for him, but the 200 metres was *his* race – and he wanted to beat the world record.

He started very quickly, and he was in front of everyone when he came out of the bend. In the last one hundred metres, he was not in a race with athletes – he was in a race with the clock. Usain did not relax and open his arms this time. He raced very hard to the finish. He had a second gold medal, and his time of 19.30 seconds broke Michael Johnson's world record!

'I am Number One!'[3] he said. Then, with the national flag around him, Usain did a Jamaican dance. He got his 200 metres gold medal the next day, on his twenty-second birthday.

Usain's last race was the final of the men's 4x100 metres relay, with Jamaicans Nesta Carter, Michael Frater, and Asafa Powell – and Jamaica finished first in a world-record time.

Usain now had three Olympic gold medals, and he was the only person in any sport with three world records from one Olympics! When the Games finished, he was the most famous athlete in the world. People all around the world began doing his lightning bolt pose – and putting their photos on the internet.

Usain arrived home from Beijing in September, and thousands of people met him at the airport. Thousands more stood on the streets of Kingston in the rain, and cheered when he drove past.

With the Jamaican flag
after the 200 metres, Beijing

Gold medal for the 200 metres, Beijing

**Usain at the Sherwood Content party**

Two weeks later, the villagers of Sherwood Content had a big party for Usain. Famous Jamaican singers were there, and people ate, sang, and danced into the night.

After Beijing, Usain had millions of fans around the world. He was very famous now, so he was on TV a lot, and lots of businesses wanted to work with him. They gave him money when he did things for them or wore their running shoes or shirts.

When Usain first began racing at big championships, he looked at Asafa Powell with his expensive car and thought, *One day, I want that*. Now he was rich and he had a nice car, too. He could have fun. But he did not forget his old friends and family, or his country. He helped his mother and father with his money, and he lived with his brother Sadiki. His best friend NJ worked with him later, and when Usain could, he always helped Jamaican businesses.

# 8  Yohan Blake

In April 2009, Usain was with two friends in his expensive new car on a road near Kingston. It began to rain, and suddenly the car hit some water and went off the road. It turned over and over. Coach Mills saw pictures of the accident on TV, and the car looked very bad. *Usain is dead*, he thought at first.

Usain went to hospital with his friends. They were all OK, but later, Usain thought a lot about the accident. *Why didn't I die?* he thought. It changed him: he wanted to do important things with his time now.

Usain began helping athletes at his club. When he saw young runners there, he talked to them and taught them important things. He often took money to the track when he trained, too, and gave it to people when they asked him for help.

Usain had injuries to his feet from his car accident, but they did not stop him getting new world records for the 100 metres and 200 metres at the World Championships in Berlin in August 2009. After that, he wanted a quiet year. So in 2010, he trained and did some races, but he relaxed and went to lots of parties, too.

He began training hard again in 2011, but after his quiet year, he needed to do a lot of work – and there was a new athlete at Usain's club in Kingston now. Yohan Blake was three years younger than Usain, very strong, and very

Yohan Blake

fast. Blake loved cricket, and he and Usain were soon good friends.

Blake was different from Usain. He always worked very, very hard in training. He never stopped because he was tired. He wanted to be a champion – and he wanted to beat Usain.

At the World Championships in Daegu, South Korea, in August 2011, Usain made a false start in the 100 metres final – by accident, he began running before the start of the race. When an athlete does this, they must leave the track. So after months of training, Usain was out of the race. He could not believe it! Yohan Blake won the race and was the new 100 metres World Champion. Usain won the final of the 200 metres at Daegu – but he could not stop thinking about his false start in the 100 metres.

Usain's false start, Daegu, 2011

For the Olympics, countries have trials – they have races and find the best athletes. At the Jamaican trials for the 2012 London Olympics, Blake beat Usain in the 100 metres and the 200 metres. *Blake is the champion now, not Usain*, people in Jamaica began to say.

But Usain did not think that. He wanted two things now: he wanted to win at the Olympics, and he wanted to beat Blake.

When Usain arrived in London for the 2012 Olympics, he could not go out of the Olympic village – because everyone knew his face, and all his fans wanted to meet him. Lots of people wanted Usain to win medals, but there were some very good runners in the races that year: Yohan Blake, of course, and the American runners Tyson Gay and Justin Gatlin, too.

Usain with the Jamaican flag at the start of the London 2012 Olympics

On 5th August, Usain went out onto the track for the 100 metres final. He did not start well, but soon he was next to Blake and the Americans. Then his long legs began to carry him away from them. His time of 9.63 seconds was a new Olympic record, and Usain was very happy – he was the best in the world again. He ran around the track with the Jamaican flag, waved at the crowd, then did his famous lightning bolt pose.

Four days later, Usain won the 200 metres race, too: now he was the best runner of all time in the 100 metres and the 200 metres. And when the Jamaican team, with Usain, won the 4x100 metres relay in the last days of the Games, he got his sixth Olympic gold medal.

The Jamaican relay team,
London

# 9 The last Olympics

When Usain began training for his fourth Olympics – the 2016 Games in Rio de Janeiro – he was twenty-nine. Training was harder for him now, and he had more injuries, too. After races and training, he often needed to sit in very cold water, for his tired legs and body.

Usain training for the 2016 Olympics

Usain worked hard off the track, too, because he was very famous. Sometimes he needed to forget everything and relax, so he went out with his friends and danced, or went home and stayed with his mother and father in Sherwood Content. There, he was a famous athlete second – and he was Jennifer's boy Usain first.

Usain's fans loved him, and when he arrived in Brazil for the 2016 Olympics, everyone wanted to talk to him. Usain was the world's fastest man – but he liked to laugh and have fun, too. So when he talked to people from the TV and newspapers one day, he answered their questions, and then did a Brazilian dance called the samba!

Usain had a lot of injuries in 2014 and 2015, and before the Olympics, the American Justin Gatlin had the fastest time for the 100 metres. In the final, on 14th August, Gatlin started faster than Usain – but after fifty metres, Usain went past Gatlin. Then he relaxed, and before he got to the finish, he hit his hands on his body excitedly. *It's my race*, that said. People cheered and waved. Eight years after the Beijing Olympics, no one was faster than Usain Bolt!

Usain talks to people before the 2016 Rio Olympics

Usain with the crowd, Rio

The 200 metres was a great race for Usain, too. He had a wonderful start, and he was in front when he came out of the bend. Canadian Andre de Grasse was very fast in the last one hundred metres of the race, but he could not beat Usain. Later, Usain ran in the 4x100 metres relay, and the Jamaican team won the gold medal for that race, too. Usain now had nine gold medals from three Olympics.

4x100 metres relay medals, Rio

With his 200 metres medal, Rio

The evening after the relay, Usain stayed in the stadium with his friends. He wanted to do the javelin, for fun. It was late, and there were not many people in the stadium, but he waved at the little crowd. Then he ran across the track, his arms went out, and the javelin left his hand. It went fifty-six metres – not bad for a beginner!

# 10 The world's fastest man

In August 2017, Usain started around the track in London one last time. He did not run, he walked; and the crowd cheered for their hero.

This was Usain's 'goodbye' to his fans, and to racing, after his last championships. He did not win his races at the World Championships in London that summer, but it did not matter. Today, people do not think of those races when they remember Usain – they think of the fun, fast champion, and his Olympic gold medals.

When Usain walked around the London stadium, he waved to the crowd, and did his lightning bolt pose – and on the track's clock, everyone could see his world record times. He stopped at the start of the 100 metres and 200 metres, and said 'goodbye'.

Usain's 'goodbye' to racing, London, 2017

**Usain with his mother and father, London, 2017**

Usain was the world's best athlete for ten years, but now he wanted to do something new. What a wonderful ten years! Between 2008 and 2017, he raced 169 times – and won more than 150 of those races! He was the Laureus Sportsman of the Year four times and the IAAF World Athlete of the Year six times. And when he stopped racing in 2017, he had the 100, 200, and 4x100 metres world records.

Perhaps Usain Bolt is the greatest athlete of all time – but the fans loved him most because he was fun, and always had time for people. When someone wanted to meet Usain, he always liked to stop and talk to them.

After he stopped running, Usain often visited schools in Jamaica and around the world, and he talked to children about sport and his work in athletics. He began playing a lot of football, too. Usain started an organization called the Usain Bolt Foundation, and it helps schools, sports clubs, and young people. Usain helps his village, Sherwood Content, a lot, too, and every Christmas, he has a big party there. There are sports and games for children, and people dance and eat Jamaican food.

Sherwood Content has a lot of visitors these days. People from all around the world come and take photos of Jennifer and Wellesley Bolt's home, and Aunt Lilly's house. And they stop people on the street and ask 'Do you know Usain Bolt?'

From Kingston, the road to Sherwood Content goes through the green hills of Jamaica. You drive past little villages with tall trees and houses of many colours. Children play cricket, and animals walk on the road. Two and a half hours later, you drive into Usain's village, Sherwood Content – home of the world's fastest man: Usain Bolt.

Usain plays football for Soccer Aid, England, 2018

**around** *(prep)*  in different places; on all sides of something

**athletics** *(n)*  a sport: running, jumping, etc.; **athlete** *(n)*  An athlete does athletics.

**aunt** *(n)*  the sister of your mother or father, or the wife of their brother

**award** *(n)*  a prize or money; you give it to somebody who has done something very well

**beat** *(v)*  to do something faster or better than another person or people; to arrive before another person or people

**believe** *(v)*  to think that something is true

**bend** *(n)*  Something with a bend in it goes to the left or right.

**birthday** *(n)*  the day you were born

**bucket** *(n)*  a round thing for carrying something, e.g. water

**business** *(n)*  a shop, factory, etc.; it makes or sells things

**champion** *(n)*  the best person at something, e.g. running, football, or tennis; **championship** *(n)*  a day/days when lots of people do a sport or game, and everyone wants to win

**cheer** *(v)*  to make a loud noise because you are happy or something is good

**chicken nugget** *(n)*  a small piece of meat; it is a 'fast food' and you can eat it with your hands

**club** *(n)*  when people meet every day, week, etc. and do something together, e.g. a sport

**cricket** *(n)*  a game; players hit a ball and run

**crowd** *(n)*  a lot of people

**dance** *(v & n)*  to move your body to music

**exercise** *(n)*  moving your body again and again in the same way because you want to be well or do a sport better

**final** *(n)*  the last game or race in a championship

**flag** *(n)*  a piece of cloth or paper with special colours or pictures for a country

**food** *(n)*  People and animals eat food.

**fun** *(n)*  People laugh and have a good time when things are fun.

**game** *(n)*  A game has rules (things that you must or cannot do), and people play it; a big championship, e.g. the Olympics.

**gold** *(adj)*  an expensive yellow metal; the medal for the winner of a big championship

**great** *(adj)*  very, very good

**hard** *(adj & adv)*  not easy; with a lot of work

**hero** *(n)*  A hero does something good or very hard.

**injury** *(n)*  when you hurt (cut, break, etc.) a part of the body

**javelin** *(n)*  a sport in athletics: you throw a long stick

**lightning bolt** *(n)*  a moment of lightning (a sudden light in the sky when there is a storm)

**medal** *(n)*  A medal is round and made of metal; you get it when you do something very good, e.g. win a championship.

**newspaper** *(n)*  You read a newspaper. It tells you what is happening in the world/your country/your town.

**organization** *(n)*  In an organization, a group of people work together.

**pose** *(n)*  how someone stands or sits when a person takes a photograph of them

**race** *(n & v)*  In a race, people want to run, drive, etc. the fastest.

**record** *(n)*  the fastest time in a race

**relax** *(v)*  to not work; to not use your body

**relay** *(n)*  a race with more than one part; every person in a team runs, walks, etc. one of the parts

**sport** *(n)*  a game or activity, e.g. football or running

**stadium** *(n)*  In a stadium, you can sit and watch sport.

**start** *(v & n)*  to begin to do something

**strong** *(adj)*  A strong person can carry big things.

**team** *(n)*  a group of people playing or working together in a sport or a game

**track** *(n)*  a special road for races

**train** *(v)*  to do something a lot because you want to be good at it; **training** *(n)*  how or when you train for something

**university** *(n)*  a place for learning, after you leave high school

**wave** *(v)*  to move your hand because you want to say hello or goodbye

**win** *(v)*  to be the best or the first in a game, race, or sport

**world** *(n)*  the Earth with all its countries and people

North Atlantic Ocean
THE BAHAMAS
CUBA
CAYMAN ISLANDS
TURKS & CAICOS ISLANDS
JAMAICA
Kingston
See page 3
HAITI
DOMINICAN REPUBLIC
PUERTO RICO
US VIRGIN ISLANDS
BRITISH VIRGIN ISLANDS
ANGUILLA
ST KITTS & NEVIS
ANTIGUA & BARBUDA
GUADELOUPE
DOMINICA
MARTINIQUE
ST LUCIA
ST VINCENT & THE GRENADINES
BARBADOS
GRENADA
TRINIDAD & TOBAGO
ARUBA
CURACAO
Caribbean Sea
N
0
200
400km

# The life of Usain Bolt

| | |
|---|---|
| **1986** | • Born in Sherwood Content, Jamaica, on 21st August. |
| **1998** | • Goes to William Knibb High School, in Falmouth, Jamaica. |
| **2001** | • Wins the 400 metres race at the National Boys and Girls Championships ('Champs'). |
| **2002** | • Wins the 200 metres final at the World Junior Championships. |
| **2004** | • Goes to the Athens Olympics, but has an injury and does not run well. |
| **2008** | • Wins gold medals for the 100 metres, 200 metres, and 4x100 metres relay at the Beijing Olympics, and breaks all three world records. |
| **2009** | • Has a car accident.<br>• Breaks his 100 metres and 200 metres world records at the Berlin World Championships. |
| **2012** | • Wins three gold medals at the London Olympics. |
| **2016** | • Wins three gold medals at the Rio Olympics. He now has nine Olympic gold medals. |
| **2017** | • Stops racing after the London World Championships. |

# Important people in Usain's life

**Jennifer and Wellesley Bolt** are Usain's mother and father. Usain did not like being away from them, and they went to all his important races.

**Nugent Walker Junior**, or NJ, is Usain's best friend. They met when they were four years old. NJ now helps Usain with his business.

**Glen Mills** was Usain's coach at his athletics club in Kingston. Mills began training Usain in 2004, after he had a bad leg injury.

**Yohan Blake** trained with Usain, and he is one of the world's best 100 and 200 metres athletes. Usain worked harder because Yohan Blake wanted to beat him.

# Usain Bolt: the best in the world

**Olympic Champion** | Usain won nine Olympic gold medals

100 metres · 200 metres · 4x100 metres relay*
**BEIJING 2008**

100 metres · 200 metres · 4x100 metres relay
**LONDON 2012**

100 metres · 200 metres · 4x100 metres relay
**RIO 2016**

*The Jamaican 4x100 metres relay team later lost this medal.*

**World Champion** | Usain won eleven gold medals at the World Championships

**BERLIN 2009** · **DAEGU 2011** · **MOSCOW 2013** · **BEIJING 2015**

**World Records** | When he stopped racing, Usain had three world records

9.58 SECONDS
100 metres
**BERLIN 2009**

19.19 SECONDS
200 metres
**BERLIN 2009**

36.84 SECONDS
4x100 metres relay
(with Nesta Carter, Michael Frater, and Yohan Blake)
**LONDON 2012**

**How fast was he?**

Usain Bolt could run at

## 44.72 kilometres an hour!*

* *That's 12.4 metres a second!*

## Think ahead

1 Look at the back cover and the contents page. Tick (✓) the things you think you are going to read about in this book.

| | | | |
|---|---|---|---|
| being famous | ☐ | medals | ☐ |
| computers | ☐ | races | ☐ |
| doctors | ☐ | school friends | ☐ |
| family | ☐ | running | ☐ |
| football | ☐ | travel | ☐ |
| Jamaican food | ☐ | | |

2 How much do you know about Usain Bolt? Which sentences are correct?

1 Usain Bolt's family were rich.
2 Usain played cricket when he was young.
3 He had many injuries.
4 His coach did not want him to run the 100 metres.
5 He has two brothers.
6 He is more than two metres tall.

3 **RESEARCH** Before you read, find the answers to these questions.

1 Where and when was Usain Bolt born?
2 When did he become World Junior Champion?
3 How many times was he in the Jamaican Olympic team?

# Chapter check

**CHAPTER 1** **Complete the text with the numbers.**

*0.08   3   4   8   40   60   100*

It is August 2016 and Usain Bolt is in the men's
[1]_____________ metres final. There are [2]_____________
runners in the race, and [3]_____________ thousand people
are watching in the stadium.
In the first [4]_____________ seconds of the race, Usain goes
past [5]_____________ runners. Now he is running at about
[6]_____________ kilometres an hour. Usain goes in front of
Justin Gatlin and wins the race by [7]_____________ seconds.

**CHAPTER 2** **Are the sentences true or false?**

1  Usain never sat down for long when he was young.
2  Usain's father made dresses for people.
3  Usain was strong because he carried a lot of water.
4  His best friend at school was Sadiki.
5  Usain liked cricket and was good at it.
6  A teacher wanted Usain to run in a race at sports day,
    but he did not win.

**CHAPTER 3** Put the events in the correct order, 1–6.

a  Usain loses some races to Keith Spence.
b  Usain beats Ricardo Geddes.
c  Usain starts at William Knibb High School.
d  Usain beats Keith Spence.
e  Usain runs in his first national championships.
f  Usain watches a video of the Atlanta Olympics.

**CHAPTER 4** Complete the sentences with one word from the chapter.

1  The biggest school athletics championships in the ______________ is called 'Champs'.
2  Usain won the 400 ______________ race at Champs.
3  In 2001, he ______________ Jamaica for the first time and went to Barbados.
4  The next year, in Nassau, the crowd cheered him and called him '______________ Bolt'.
5  At the World Junior Championships, Usain did not want to ______________ in front of the Jamaican crowd.
6  After he became World Junior Champion, Usain was a ______________ in Jamaica.

**CHAPTER 5** Answer the questions with the words.

*2003    April 2004    Asafa Powell*
*Glen Mills    his back    his leg*

1  When did Usain go to university?
2  When did he break the world junior 200 metres record?
3  What did he injure later that year?
4  Where was the bend in Usain's body?
5  Who trained Usain after Athens?
6  Which Jamaican athlete made a lot of money from
   the sport?

**CHAPTER 6** Are the statements true, false, or not
mentioned in the text?

1  Usain wanted to train for the 400 metres, but Glen Mills
   wanted him to do the 100 metres.
2  Before Usain tried the new race, he needed to break the
   national record for the 200 metres.
3  Usain came second in his 100 metres race in Greece.
4  Asafa Powell ran in the 100 metres in the New York
   championships.
5  Usain broke the world record in his fifth 100 metres race.

**CHAPTER 7** Match the sentence halves. Then complete a–e with one word.

1  When Usain went to China for the 2008 Olympics, …
2  91,000 people watched…
3  When Usain won the race, people in Jamaica…
4  In the 200 metres final, Usain…
5  When Usain arrived back in Jamaica, …

a  had a race with the ______________, not the athletes.
b  he made a ______________ on his phone about winning three gold medals.
c  thousands of people ______________ him at the airport.
d  the Olympic men's 100 metres ______________ in Beijing.
e  ______________ in the streets.

**CHAPTER 8** Put the events in the correct order, 1–6.

a  Blake beats Usain in the Olympic trials in Jamaica.
b  Usain gets his sixth Olympic gold medal.
c  Usain breaks an Olympic record in the 100 metres race.
d  Blake becomes the new World Champion.
e  Usain has an accident in his car.
f  Usain makes a false start at the World Championships.

**CHAPTER 9** Complete the sentences with the correct names. Use some names more than once.

*Andre de Grasse    Justin Gatlin    Usain Bolt*

1 ______________ was twenty-nine when he began training for the Rio Olympics.

2 ______________ had the fastest 100 metres time in 2016 before the Rio Olympics.

3 ______________ started faster than Usain in the 100 metres final.

4 ______________ was very fast in the 200 metres, but he could not beat Usain.

5 After the 4x100 metres relay, ______________ did the javelin.

**CHAPTER 10** Correct the <u>underlined</u> words.

1 In London in August 2017, Usain <u>won</u> his last races.
2 Usain was the best athlete in the world for <u>eight</u> years.
3 Usain stopped racing in <u>2018</u>.
4 Usain had three <u>national</u> records when he stopped racing.
5 Every Christmas, Usain has a big <u>championship</u> in Sherwood Content.
6 Usain's village is two and a half hours from <u>Sherwood Content</u>.

# Focus on vocabulary

1 **Match the words to the definitions.**

*champion   coach   medal   pose   record   stadium*

1  Athletes get this when they come first, second, or third in a race.
2  This person helps athletes when they are training.
3  How you stand when someone takes your photo.
4  This place has a track, and you watch athletes run here.
5  The fastest time in the world for a race.
6  The best person at a sport, e.g. running.

2 **Complete what the TV speakers say with the words below.**

*beat   crowd   fans   final   track*

The great man, Usain Bolt, is coming out onto the
1_____________ for the 2_____________ of the men's 100
metres. He's got 3_____________ all over the world, of course,
and most people in the 4_____________ of 60,000 here tonight
want him to win. But there are very good athletes in this
race. Can he 5_____________ them?

*club   exercises   races   team   train*

I'm here at the Racers Track 6_____________ in Kingston,
Jamaica. Jamaican Olympic 7_____________ runners Usain
Bolt and Yohan Blake 8_____________ here six days a
week with their coach Glen Mills. They do 9_____________
for their legs, arms, and backs every day, and they run
10_____________ around the track again and again.

# Focus on language

1  **Complete the two extracts from Chapter 8 with
the prepositions.**

*in   in   near   off   on*

¹_____________ April 2009, Usain was with two friends
²_____________ his expensive new car ³_____________ a road
⁴_____________ Kingston. It began to rain, and <u>suddenly</u> the
car hit some water <u>and</u> went ⁵_____________ the road.

*around   at   away   in   next to   on   out*

⁶_____________ 5ᵗʰ August, Usain went ⁷_____________ onto
the track for the 100 metres final. He did not start well,
<u>but</u> soon he was ⁸_____________ Blake and the Americans.
<u>Then</u> his long legs began to carry him ⁹_____________ from
them. His time of 9.63 seconds was a new Olympic record,
and Usain was very happy – he was the best ¹⁰_____________
the world again. He ran ¹¹_____________ the track with the
Jamaican flag, waved ¹²_____________ the crowd, then did
his famous lightning bolt pose.

2  **DECODE** **Look at the <u>underlined</u> words in the extracts
above. Which word…**

1  says what happened next?
2  says that something happened quickly?
3  adds an extra phrase or information?
4  adds some information that is very different?

## Discussion

1  Read the question and then look at the dialogue. Which two speakers agree in the end?

What was Usain Bolt's best Olympic Games?

ENRIQUE: Hmm… <u>I think that</u> London 2012 was great. Yohan Blake beat Usain in the Olympic trials for the Jamaican team, but Usain came back and won three gold medals.

KEIRA: <u>Good point</u>. <u>What about you</u>, Max?

MAX: The Rio Olympics was Usain's best Games – because he was nearly thirty years old in Rio, but he beat the best athletes in the world. <u>What do you think</u>, Keira?

KEIRA: <u>For me</u>, it was the Beijing Olympics. When he ran in the 100 metres, it looked easy!

MAX: <u>That's true</u>. He did the lightning bolt pose for the first time in Beijing, too. Yes, <u>on second thoughts,</u> Beijing was the best.

2  Read the dialogue in exercise 1 again. Look at the <u>underlined</u> phrases. Which phrase/phrases do the speakers use…

- to ask for opinions?
- to agree with someone?
- to give opinions?
- to change opinion?

3  **THINK CRITICALLY**  Read the question below. What is your answer, and why?

What is the world's best sports championship?
Is it…

a  the FIFA Football World Cup?
b  the Olympic Games?
c  another championship? (Please say what this is.)

4  **COMMUNICATE**  Talk about the question in exercise 3 with one or two partners. Use the phrases from exercise 2.

1 **Read the text about the athlete Cathy Freeman. Which race did Cathy Freeman and Usain Bolt both win a gold medal for?**

Cathy Freeman was born in the town of Mackay in Queensland, Australia in 1973. She loved running when she was a child, and she won an 80 metres school championship race when she was only eight.

Cathy's parents were poor Aboriginal people and they could not buy her running shoes. Because of this, white Australian athletes sometimes laughed at Cathy. But in 1988, she started at a school in Queensland with very good athletics training.

In 1990, Cathy went to the Commonwealth Games in New Zealand. She ran in the 4x100 metres relay and won her first international gold medal. Then, in the Olympics in Sydney in 2000, she won a gold medal in the 400 metres.

In 2007, she started the Cathy Freeman Foundation. It helps Aboriginal families and children all over Australia.

**Aboriginal** *(adj)*  the people in Australia before Europeans arrived

**Commonwealth** *(n)*  a group of English-speaking countries

2 Complete the second column of the table about Cathy Freeman's life.

| Name | Cathy Freeman |
|---|---|
| Born (where and when) | |
| Began sport (what and when) | |
| Being a sportsperson was hard because... | |
| Important championships and medals | |
| Other interests / work | |

3 (COLLABORATE) In pairs, choose an interesting sportsperson and find out about them. Copy the table in exercise 2, and complete it with information about that sportsperson.

4 (CREATE) In your pair, practise a short presentation about the person you chose in exercise 3. Give your presentation to the class.

# If you liked this Bookworm, why not try...

## Brazil

STAGE 1
Nick Bullard

Everyone knows about Brazil's beautiful beaches, the Amazon rainforest, and the wonderful Carnival of Rio de Janeiro. But there is a lot more to Brazil than this: here you can find interesting old towns, modern cities, and thousands of different kinds of animals and plants. It is home to world-famous artists and writers, and international sporting events like the World Cup and the Olympics, too.

What other interesting things can you see here? Why is there music and dancing on its streets? And who are the people of this amazing country?

---

## John Lennon

STAGE 1
Alex Raynham

'One day, I'm going to be famous,' John Lennon said when he was young – and soon he was! His band The Beatles became one of the greatest in the world, and people loved them.

After John Lennon went solo, he wrote some of the most important songs of all time. He was a family man and a peace protestor – he wanted to change the world. But one autumn day, four gun shots rang out across New York, and took away that dream for ever...